Amazing Animal Hunters
WOLVES

Jen Green

amicus

Published by Amicus
P.O. Box 1329, Mankato, Minnesota 56002

Printed in the United States of America at Corporate Graphics, in North Mankato, Minnesota.

Library of Congress Cataloging-in-Publication Data
Green, Jen.
  Wolves / by Jen Green.
      p. cm. -- (Amazing animal hunters)
  Includes index.
  Summary: "Discusses the life of wolves and profiles different species of wolves, including
where they live, what they eat, and more. Provides facts and records on wolves"--Provided by publisher.
  ISBN 978-1-60753-050-3 (library binding)
  1. Wolves--Juvenile literature. I. Title.
  QL737.C22G7254 2011
  599.773--dc22

                                                                        2009047604

Created by Q2AMedia
Editor: Katie Dicker
Art Director: Harleen Mehta
Designer: Dibakar Acharjee and Shilpi Sarkar
Picture Researcher: Maria Janet
Line Artist: Rama Krishna
Colouring Artist: Abhijeet Sharma

Picture credits
t=top b=bottom c=center l=left r=right
Cover images: Zorro/Dreamstime, Dreamstime

Denis Pepin/Istockphoto: Title page, Amanda Rohde/Istockphoto: Contents page, Motor-Presse Syndication/Photolibrary: 4,
Tanya Kozlovsky/Shutterstock: 5, Ronald Wittek/Photolibrary: 6, Thomas Kitchin & Victoria Hurst/Photolibrary: 7,
David W Hamilton/Photolibrary: 8, Takiev Alexander/Shutterstock: 9t, James Urbach/Photolibrary: 9b, K Wothe/
Photolibrary: 10, Mikael Wahlberg/Photolibrary: 11t, Mike Robinson/Photolibrary: 11b, Ronald Wittek/Photolibrary: 12,
Dmitrij/Dreamstime: 13t, Joe McDonald/NHPA: 14, Mark Hamblin/Photolibrary: 15, Steven Kazlowski/Photolibrary: 16,
Michael Sewell/Photolibrary: 17, Eyal Bartov/Photolibrary: 18, T Kitchin & V Hurst/NHPA: 19, Denis Pepin/Istockphoto: 20,
Steven Kazlowski/Photolibrary: 21, Christian Heinrich/Photolibrary: 22, Gisela Delpho/Photolibrary: 23,
The Bridgeman Art Library/Photolibrary: 24, Jeff & Alexa Henry/Photolibrary: 25, Martin Harvey/Photolibrary: 26,
Mary Lee Woodward/Istockphoto: 27, FloridaStock/Shutterstock: 28, Michael DeYoung/Photolibrary: 29,
Takiev Alexander/Shutterstock: 31.

Q2AMedia Art Bank: 13.

DAD0043
42010

9 8 7 6 5 4 3 2 1

Contents

Fierce Hunters 4

Living Together 6

Case Study: Sounds and Signals 8

Fast and Fearless 10

Super Senses 12

Case Study: A Deer Hunt 14

Lonely Life 16

Desert and Forest 18

Case Study: The White Wolf 20

Raising Cubs 22

Wolves and People 24

Case Study: Rare Wolves 26

Facts and Records 28

Glossary 30

Index and Web Finder 32

Fierce Hunters

Mean and menacing, with shaggy fur and sharp teeth—that's how many people see wolves. Wolves tend to be feared as ferocious, meat-eating hunters. But wolves have a gentler side, too. They are loyal, affectionate, and among the world's most intelligent animals.

Sharp canine tooth

The Wolf Family

Wolves are **predators**—they kill other animals for food. Their main weapons are the long, pointed fangs in the front of their jaws, which they use to seize **prey**. These teeth are called canines, and they give the wolf family its name, the **canids**. Coyotes, jackals, and dingoes are closely related to the wolf. Foxes and wild dogs are more distant relatives.

When a wolf snarls, you can see its canine teeth. Wolves, wild dogs, and foxes all have long, sharp canines.

One Species

Wolves are creatures of the north. They were once found all across North America, Europe, and Asia, but now they are much rarer. There is only one **species** (or type) of wolf—the gray wolf. But gray wolves that live in different **habitats**, such as forests and deserts, look a little different from one another. Wolves are unusual in that they are able to **breed** with close relatives such as coyotes and domestic dogs. This results in cross-breeds, such as coy-wolves and wolf-dogs.

MAN'S BEST FRIEND?

People see wolves as enemies. But "man's best friend," the domestic dog, is actually descended from the wolf. Dogs were bred from wolves about 12,000 years ago. Over the centuries, people bred dogs to do different jobs, such as guarding or hunting. There are now more than 400 different dog breeds.

The wolf-like husky was bred to pull sleds in the Arctic

 All dogs—from the miniature poodle to the giant St. Bernard —are descended from the wolf.

Living Together

Wolves are very sociable creatures. Almost all wolves spend their lives in a group called a **pack**. The main purpose of the pack is for hunting. The wolf pack also provides a safe place to raise their young.

Pack Hunters

As predators, wolves go after all sorts of prey. Their favorite prey are large, hoofed animals, such as elk, moose, and caribou (reindeer). These big beasts will provide a meal for many hunters, but they are powerful, with sharp hooves and horns or antlers. Hunting in a pack allows wolves to target large prey. Single wolves could never tackle these creatures on their own.

 As part of a team, a wolf is able to kill prey up to ten times its own weight.

Pecking Order

Most packs contain eight to twelve wolves. The pack is well organized, with a strict **hierarchy** or "pecking order." The strongest, most experienced male and female are the leaders. Scientists call these the **alpha wolves**. They are the only wolves allowed to breed. The other pack members are usually their children—young **cubs** and wolves of up to three years old. Outsiders are sometimes allowed to join the pack.

The alpha male takes the lead in hunting and defending the group. He decides when and where to go hunting. The alpha female helps to keep the other wolves in line. Large packs may have another pair of wolves who are second in command. These are called **beta wolves**.

LITTLE AND LARGE

The smallest wolf packs contain just two or three animals. The largest pack ever recorded held 36 wolves. This was in Alaska, where wolves go after large prey such as caribou and musk oxen. In general, the biggest wolf packs form in areas that contain the biggest prey animals.

Wolves in a pack have strong bonds. When pack members meet, they whine, lick faces and bury their noses in each other's fur.

Sounds and Signals

Good communication is the key to success in the wolf pack. Wolves "talk" to one another using sounds, scents, and body language. Loud, eerie howls send long-distance messages.

Alpha wolves will outstare junior pack members

Body Language

Wolves use body language to show their rank within the pack. The alpha male and female stand tall with their ears pricked and heads and tails held high. Younger or weaker dogs show their junior rank by cringing with ears laid back and tails tucked between their legs. If a junior animal challenges a top wolf by snarling, the leader snarls back ferociously. The junior dog may roll on its back or beg for food to show it is backing down.

 Alpha wolves stand tall, with their ears pricked, so they look as big as possible.

Long-Distance Communication

Wolves talk to each other up close using yips, growls, barks, and other noises. Howling is used for long-distance communication. When one wolf begins to howl, all the others join in. Each animal has a different voice, so wolves can identify distant pack members. Wolves howl as they gather before hunting. They also howl to warn rival packs to stay away. The eerie howl of a wolf can carry 6 miles (10 km) or more.

Wolves lift their nose in the air to howl.

FACIAL EXPRESSIONS

Scientists have discovered that wolves have at least 20 different **facial** expressions. A wolf raises its ears and bares its teeth to threaten another. By laying its ears back and "grinning" with its teeth hidden, a junior wolf says, "I give in, you are stronger." Dogs use many of the same expressions and body language.

This wolf is baring its teeth to scare another creature away.

Fast and Fearless

Wolves are lean, strong, and tough—a deadly combination for a hunter. With their long, muscular legs, they are fast movers and almost tireless. Their powerful jaws and sharp canines are used to seize their prey.

Marathon Runners

Like all canids, wolves run on their toes. They are not the fastest sprinters, but can keep on the move for hours at a steady pace without tiring. A wolf can manage a top speed of almost 28 mph (45 km/h) for a short distance, to grab fleeing prey. Wolves can also dodge and swerve after prey such as deer and rabbits. With their strong back legs, they can clear 13-foot (4 m) fences. They are good swimmers, too, and sometimes enter water to capture their prey.

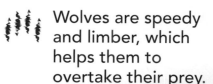 Wolves are speedy and limber, which helps them to overtake their prey.

Strong, slender legs

Bushy tail helps with balance when running

Powerful shoulders

Sleek and Deadly

Wolves have very powerful jaws and a long muzzle. As well as long canines, they have scissor-like shearing teeth at the back of their jaws. These teeth are called carnassial teeth, and they can slice through flesh. From its pointed nose to the tip of its long tail, a wolf is sleek and **streamlined**, so it can run fast through tangled undergrowth.

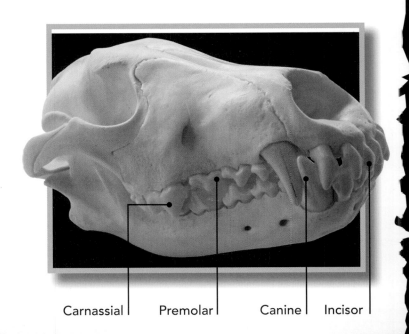

Carnassial | Premolar | Canine | Incisor

Warm Fur

The wolf's coat has two types of hairs. Long, coarse hairs called **guard hairs** keep out wind, rain, and snow. Soft, dense underfur keeps the wolf snug and warm, even in freezing temperatures.

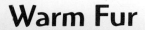 Wolves have four types of teeth: small incisors, long canines, premolars and molars to cut or crunch bone, and scissor-like carnassials.

When wolves run, they place their feet in a straight line to make a narrow trail.

ON THE RUN

A trotting wolf pack can keep up a steady pace of 27 mph (38 km/h) for hours. It is not unusual for a pack to cover 124 miles (200 km) in a day. Scientists studying one pack in Alaska found the wolves traveled 500 miles (805 km) in a month— that's about 17 miles (27 km) a day.

Super Senses

Wolves are able to hunt day or night thanks to their sharp senses. A wolf's senses are similar to those of a dog. A wolf has a very large brain to interpret all the information gathered by its senses. Dogs are intelligent, but wolves have an even bigger brain.

A World of Smells

Wolves mainly track their prey using their sharp sense of smell. The wolf's sensitive nose can identify literally thousands of different smells. Its world is a patchwork of scents that act like landmarks on a journey. The wolf remembers all these smells to build up a "scent map" in its head.

TRACKING A TRAIL

A wolf can pick up the scent of a deer 1.6 miles (2 km) away. By sniffing a scent trail, it can tell what type of animal has passed, and whether it was sick or injured. It knows how long ago it passed, and whether it was already being stalked by another wolf.

Wolves can follow the scent of its prey for many miles, even in the snow.

Eyes and Ears

Wolves are good at seeing moving objects, but find it difficult to spot an animal that "freezes" in its tracks and keeps quite still. Wolves have a wide **field of vision** to see all around. The back of their eyes also reflects light to help them to see in moonlight. If a wolf is caught in a car's headlights, its slanting eyes seem to give off an eerie glow.

Wolves can hear very high sounds that we cannot hear. This super sense allows them to hear the rustle of distant deer moving quietly through the forest. If your hearing was that good, you would be able to hear the sound of a ticking watch fifteen paces away.

 All the wolf's main senses are on its head.

Large ears swivel to catch sounds

Eyes see well in dim light

Whiskers are used for feeling at close range

Long snout contains hollow chambers that help to identify smells

Nose can identify thousands of smells

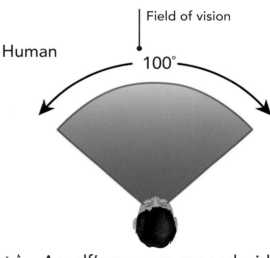

Human

Field of vision

100°

A wolf's eyes are spaced wider than a person's and set high on its head. This gives it a very wide field of vision.

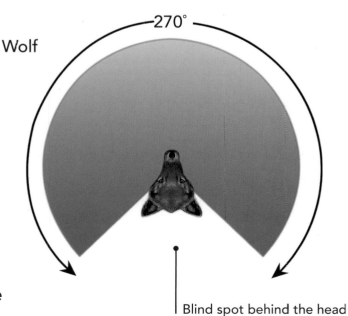

Wolf

270°

Blind spot behind the head

13

A Deer Hunt

Wolves are **carnivores**—they eat an all-meat diet if they can. If a wolf gets very hungry, it will eat plants and berries. The wolf pack acts as a team to track, stalk, chase, and finally bring down a large beast, such as an elk or a deer.

A pack of wolves chases the scent of another meal.

Stalking Prey

A pack of wolves is hunting at dusk on a snowy landscape. At last they catch the scent of a deer herd **grazing** several miles away. The wolves approach their prey cautiously, keeping to the cover of rocks and bushes. They are careful to stay upwind of the herd so the deer don't catch their scent. As they get closer, the wolves single out a young deer as an easy victim.

Closing for the Kill

Like a top sports team, the wolves take different roles in the chase that follows. A few swift wolves dart ahead to separate the deer from its herd. Flankers follow the animal as it twists and turns. As the deer begins to tire, the wolves close in. They snap at the deer's sides, and it grows weak from fear and loss of blood. Finally it trips and topples over. A strong wolf such as the alpha male kills it with a bite to the nose or throat.

RARE SUCCESS

Even hunting as a team, nine out of ten wolf hunts end in failure. The wolves will give up the chase if an animal proves too strong or speedy. They won't risk getting injured. Luckily, wolves can go for several days without food, as long as they have water to drink.

Wolves eat every part of their prey—flesh, skin, bones, and fur.

Lonely Life

Most wolves spend much of their lives in the safety of a pack, but some wolves have to survive on their own. This mostly happens when young wolves leave the group to set up a new pack. Or sometimes, an old or sickly wolf is turned out of the pack and left to fend for itself.

Struggle for Survival

For a lone wolf, life is one long struggle for survival. Without a pack, it cannot hunt large prey. So it goes after smaller creatures, such as rabbits, mice, and birds. It will also eat dead meat and fruit if very hungry. It may approach towns and villages to steal scraps from garbage dumps.

This lone wolf is feeding on a dead moose it has hidden in the snow.

SAVING IT FOR LATER

If a lone wolf is lucky enough to make a good kill, it eats its fill, and then hides the rest for later. This is called **caching**. The wolf may stash the meat under rocks or snow.

Keep Out!

Wolf packs hunt in a home area called a **territory**, where there is plenty of prey to eat. A lone wolf is not strong enough to set up a territory. It is forced to hunt in areas not taken by other wolves, where the hunting is poor. Lone wolves have to cover ten to twenty times as much ground as other wolves to find enough food.

Joining Forces

Lone wolves are shy and wary, particularly of other wolves. If a single wolf is caught in a pack's territory, the wolves may tear it to pieces. It will move quickly and quietly across pack land. In a safe, lonely spot, a lone wolf may start to howl. If another wolf answers, the pair approach cautiously. They may start a new pack together.

Wolves mark the edges of their territory with urine to warn other wolves to stay away. This is called scent-marking.

A lone wolf is always alert and wary

Desert and Forest

Gray wolves are able to live in many different habitats, including forests, deserts, mountains, grasslands, and the Arctic **tundra**. Wolves generally live in remote places where there are few people. They are tough and hardy—born survivors.

Suited to Surroundings

Wolves that live in different habitats have developed features that help them survive in their particular surroundings. Over many years, slightly different types of wolf have developed. These are called **subspecies**. Scientists have identified up to 30 subspecies of gray wolves, such as Arctic wolves, desert wolves, and forest wolves.

Large ears give off heat like mini-radiators to keep the wolf cool

Yellow eyes

Desert wolves hunt alone or in small packs to catch birds and rodents.

Bird caught as prey

Desert Wolves

Desert wolves live in dry places and rocky scrublands in Mexico and the Middle East. Their pale, tawny-colored coat blends in with the sand and rocks. The pale color also reflects sunlight, which helps to keep them cool. Desert wolves rest in the shade of rocks during the heat of the day and hunt at night when temperatures can be freezing cold.

Timber Wolves

Wolves are probably most at home in northern forests. In the U.S., forest wolves are called timber wolves. These medium-sized wolves have black, gray, pale, or reddish fur—colors that blend in with leaves and bark in the shadowy forest. Timber wolves like to hunt large prey such as moose, elk, or white-tailed deer. They also catch smaller creatures such as beavers, rabbits, and birds.

The timber wolf's fur blends in with the forest. These wolves hunt in medium-sized packs of five to ten animals.

The White Wolf

The Arctic wolf manages to survive in one of the harshest habitats on Earth—the treeless plains of the north, known as the tundra. This hostile place is covered with snow for much of the year. Winters are long, dark, and bitterly cold.

Small ears

Short snout

White fur blends in with the snow

Extra-thick winter coat keeps wolf warm

Staying Warm

Arctic wolves are bigger than other wolves. Their size helps them to keep warm in winter. Wolves in other habitats lose a lot of heat through their large ears and long noses. Arctic wolves have smaller ears and shorter snouts to reduce heat loss. In summer, the wolf sheds its winter coat for a thinner gray coat, which matches the rocks and soil.

 Arctic wolves can survive temperatures as cold as -40°F (-40°C) thanks to their dense fur.

Large Prey

Hunting can be difficult in the icy landscape, but the Arctic wolf can survive for weeks without food. Caribou and musk oxen are their favorite prey. A large pack is needed to bring down one of these powerful creatures.

Musk oxen calves make the easiest targets. But if the cattle catch the scent of a wolf pack, the adults form a circle with their babies in the middle. The musk oxen face outward with horns lowered. Faced with a wall of horns, the wolves may be forced to retreat. They may have to settle for smaller prey, such as ducks, rabbits, or rodents.

VAST TERRITORIES

The size of a pack's territory is related to the amount of prey available. In the Arctic, prey is scarce. Animals such as the caribou wander long distances, while the wolves follow. So Arctic wolves hunt in a huge area—up to 5,000 square miles (13,000 sq km). That's an area nearly half the size of Maryland.

Musk oxen calves are an Arctic wolf's favorite prey. But the long, curving horns of the adults make the hunt a risky business.

Raising Cubs

Only two animals breed in the wolf pack—the alpha male and female. If other wolves were to breed, the pack would get too big. Although the cubs are not their own, all pack members help to feed, guard, and train them.

Mating and Birth

Alpha wolves stay together for life. They breed in early spring. The pups are born two months later when the weather gets warmer. The she-wolf gives birth in a **den**—a cave or large burrow. Newborn wolves are tiny and quite helpless—they cannot see, hear, or stand. They snuggle up to their mother and drink her milk.

Growing Up

At one month old, the cubs wobble to the den entrance. They meet the rest of the pack and get their first glimpse of the outside world. They begin to eat half-chewed meat brought by the adult wolves. The cubs play in a safe place in the wolf territory. One adult guards them while the rest go hunting. At ten months old, the cubs join the hunt. At first, they just watch the adults to learn new skills.

These pups are drinking their mother's milk

Cubs have dark fuzzy fur

She-wolves usually give birth to five or six cubs, but there can be as many as a dozen.

Leaving Home

Young wolves are fully grown by 18 months old. Young she-wolves reach breeding age at two years old, males at three years old. At this point, they become a threat to their parents and are often turned out of the pack. The young wolves wander alone or with their brothers or sisters until they meet other wolves and start a new pack.

PLAY-FIGHTING

Cubs spend a lot of time play-fighting. They rarely hurt one another, but fighting establishes a pecking order that mirrors the hierarchy in the wolf pack. As two cubs wrestle, the weaker rolls on its back to show it gives up. The winner stands tall with its tail high. One day it may lead its own pack.

Fighting builds strong muscles and teaches young wolves how to behave in a pack.

Wolves have a "play-expression" to show the fight is not for real

Stronger cub

Weaker cub

Wolves and People

Wolves appear in stories and legends around the world. In fairy tales and horror films, they are shown as wicked creatures that prey on humans, especially children. But are wolves really as bad as they seem?

Big, Bad Wolf?

In real life, wolves are very wary of people and they rarely attack. Long ago, before guns were invented, they may have been bolder. Wolves tend to live far away from people, but they have been known to raid farms to steal chickens, sheep, or calves. For this reason, farmers see wolves as enemies.

Wolves Under Threat

Over the centuries, wolves have been shot, poisoned, trapped, and hunted with dogs. They have been killed for their fur, and sometimes for sport. Wolves are also put at risk when people take over the wild places where they live. In many areas, forests have been chopped down and wild grasslands fenced off to make fields and pastures. This means the wolves have less room to hunt and roam.

 This medieval illustration shows a wolf hunt. Noblemen on horses, helpers on foot, and a pack of dogs are chasing a wolf.

Bring Back the Wolf

Wolves were once common throughout the north. Now they have been wiped out in many places, including the United States, Britain, and most of western Europe. Recently, however, wolves have started to make a comeback. People's attitudes toward wolves have changed. Rather than being seen as pests, many people now admire wolves for qualities such as loyalty. Wolves bred in zoos have been released in some national parks in North America. For many people, wolves are a symbol of the wild. Like wild places, they are in need of our protection.

COYOTE COMEBACK

As wolves have been wiped out in the United States, coyotes have taken their place. About half the size of wolves, coyotes have very flexible feeding habits. They have now spread through much of North America, and even live close to towns. But they, too, steal chickens and sheep, and cause just as much trouble for farmers.

This Canadian wolf is being measured before it is released in Yellowstone National Park, to bring wolves back to the area.

Rare Wolves

Wolves were once the most widespread predator on land. Now some types of gray wolves, such as Mexican and Indian wolves, are in danger of dying out. Two close relatives of gray wolves, Simien wolves and red wolves, are also extremely rare.

Simien Wolves

Simien wolves live in the highlands of Ethiopia in East Africa. This slim, coyote-sized wolf has a handsome reddish coat and long legs. Simien wolves mostly hunt alone, killing rabbits and rodents, but may band together to kill antelope. Unlike gray wolves, which mate within their pack, Simien wolves usually mate with animals from neighboring packs.

Simien wolves are under threat because farmers have taken over the wild land where they live. People also shoot them for their fur or because they kill farm animals. Only a few hundred are left. Luckily, they mostly live in protected areas where hunting is forbidden.

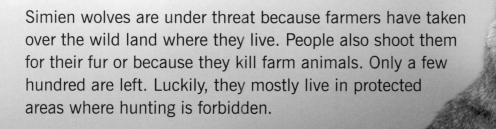

There are only about 400 Simien wolves left in the wild. The fight is on to save this rare animal.

Simien wolves are also known as Ethiopian wolves

The Red Wolf

Another very rare wolf, the red wolf, comes from North America. It was once found throughout the southeastern United States. Settlers shot large numbers of red wolves because they threatened their farm animals. By the 1970s, this wolf was **extinct** in the wild, but a few were left in zoos. In the 1980s, wolf-lovers launched a campaign to save it. Red wolves were bred in zoos, and the young were released in two protected areas. There are now about 150 of these rare wolves.

MYSTERY IDENTITY?

Scientists disagree about the true nature of the red wolf. Some experts see it as a separate species, a cousin of the gray wolf. Others think it is a crossbreed between gray wolves and coyotes—in other words, a coy-wolf.

Red wolves live in protected areas in the wild.

Facts and Records

Wolves may not be the world's fastest or largest predators, but they are among the most intelligent. Hunting in a pack, wolves are able to take on just about any creature they meet.

The Arctic wolf's thick fur and big body help it to keep warm in the cold winters.

Largest and Smallest

- The biggest gray wolf is the Arctic wolf. It measures up to 6.5 feet (2 m) long and can weigh 176 pounds (80 kg).

- The smallest gray wolves are steppe wolves and Arabian wolves. They measure about 2.6 feet (0.8 m) long and can weigh as little as 26.5 pounds (12 kg).

Giant Wolves

Around 2 million years ago, huge wolves roamed North America. The dire wolf was one-and-a-half times the size of an average gray wolf. Packs of these fierce predators hunted prehistoric camels, rhinos, and bison on grassy plains.

Body Facts

- Wolf pups are born blind and deaf. Over half of wolf pups may not survive.

- A wolf's sense of smell is over 100 times greater than that of a human.

- Wolves can't sweat because they don't have sweat glands. If a wolf gets hot, it pants with its mouth open and its long, wet tongue hanging out. Moisture evaporates from the tongue and wet nose. This helps the wolf keep cool.

These wolf pups will be very dependent on their mother for the first few months of life.

Did You Know?

- Each wolf has an individual scent. As wolves roam in search of prey, they scent-mark their route with urine. By sniffing the trail of another wolf, a pack member can probably tell which animal it is following.

- With their large stomachs, wolves can eat up to 20 lbs. (9 kg) of meat at once. That's like eating a huge turkey on your own in one sitting!

Names and Numbers

- The alpha male and female are the leaders of a wolf pack. "Alpha" is the first letter of the Greek alphabet.

- Wolves are often on the move for 8–10 hours a day.

- Arctic wolves are able to survive up to five months of darkness a year.

Glossary

alpha wolves
the name given to the top male and female in a wolf pack, who lead the others and are usually the only wolves that breed

beta wolves
wolves who are second-in-command in a wolf pack

body language
when an animal holds its body in a certain way to express its feelings or status in a group

breed
to have young; also a type of animal, such as a dog, which has been developed by breeding over many years

caching
when an animal hides food for later

canid
a member of the dog and wolf family

carnivore
an animal that eats meat

cub
a young wolf; wolf cubs are also called pups

den
the home of an animal such as a wolf

extinct
no longer in existence, having died out

facial
to do with the face

field of vision
the area an animal can see without turning its head

grazing
eating grass

guard hair
one of the long, coarse hairs that make up the outer layer of a wolf's coat

habitat
a particular place where plants and animals live, such as a forest or desert

hierarchy
a strict order within a group in which a leader makes decisions for others

pack
a group of wolves
that live and
hunt together

predator
an animal that hunts
others for food

prey
an animal that is
eaten for food
by another

species
a particular type
of animal, such
as a gray wolf

streamlined
a smooth,
pointed shape

subspecies
a subgroup within
a species, such as
desert wolves

territory
an area where
an animal lives,
hunts, and breeds,
and which it may
defend against
others of its kind

tundra
the treeless plains
of the far north

Index

alpha wolves 7, 8, 15, 22, 29

Arctic wolves 18, 20, 21, 28, 29

Asia 5

beta wolves 7

body language 8, 9, 23

caching 16

communication 8, 9, 17

cubs 7, 22, 23, 29

desert wolves 18, 19, 28

dogs 4, 5, 8, 9, 12, 24

ears 8, 9, 13, 18, 20

Europe 5, 25

eyes 13, 18

forest wolves 18, 19

fur 4, 7, 11, 19, 20, 22, 24, 26, 28

habitat 5, 18, 19, 20, 24, 26

hunting 4, 5, 6, 7, 9, 10, 12, 14, 15, 16, 17, 18, 19, 21, 22, 24, 26, 28

jaws 4, 10, 11

lone wolf 16, 17, 18, 23, 26

North America 5, 19, 25, 27, 28

noses 7, 9, 11, 12, 13, 15, 20, 29

pack 6, 7, 8, 9, 11, 14, 16, 17, 18, 19, 21, 22, 23, 26, 28, 29

prey 4, 6, 7, 10, 12, 14, 15, 16, 17, 18, 19, 21, 24, 25, 28, 29

red wolves 26, 27

running 10, 11

scent-marking 17, 29

senses 8, 12, 13, 14, 22, 29

Simien wolves 26

tails 8, 10, 11, 23

teeth 4, 9, 11

territory 17, 21, 22

threats 24, 25, 26, 27

Web Finder

Defenders of Wildlife
www.defenders.org/programs_and_policy/wildlife_conservation/imperiled_species/wolves/wolf_facts
All you need to know about wolves and how you can help to save them.

International Wolf Center
www.wolf.org/wolves/learn/justkids/kids.asp
Learn all about wolves and try out some fun wolf activities.

Wolf Park Kids!
www.wolfparkkids.org/animals/wolfstuff.html
Find out more about wolves, and try your hand at some wolf games.

Wolfquest
www.wolfquest.org
Live the life of a wild wolf in the United States with this web-based video game.

Wolfweb
www.wolfweb.com/facts.html
Find out about wolves from the past, and how these creatures live today.